Rufus King

Rufus King in the Development of Cincinnati During the Last Fifty Years

Rufus King

Rufus King in the Development of Cincinnati During the Last Fifty Years

ISBN/EAN: 9783337241681

Printed in Europe, USA, Canada, Australia, Japan

Cover: Foto ©ninafisch / pixelio.de

More available books at **www.hansebooks.com**

RUFUS KING

IN THE

Development of Cincinnati

DURING THE

LAST FIFTY YEARS

Printed for Private Distribution

CINCINNATI
ROBERT CLARKE & CO
1891

RUFUS KING.

AN attempt will not be made to write in detail a record of the life of Rufus King. His life was too full and complete to line it out on paper for perusal. It was a perfectly fulfilled life among men—a character completely developed in every part, and the most important and beautiful side is not for the public eye.

The controlling influence over the whole man—the motive power of every act, was his religious life, shown in every path, but brightest in the quiet and calm of his home. If nothing else would prevent an invasion into this sanctuary, the great aversion he himself had to proclaiming the sacred things of the inner life would arrest the active pen; but to condense into a monumental record the life of Rufus King as identified with the growth and development of Cincinnati in the last fifty years, "to hold together what he was and what he has done," is another thing. In each work in which he was engaged, its records will show his name and his efficient work, but all persons have not access to those records, and it seems a duty to bring together, in such form as even our children may read, the varied labors and the complete success of one whose name should never die, and whose example should leave its impress on generations to come.

Rufus King was born on the 30th of May, 1817, in Chillicothe, Ohio. His father was Edward King, fourth son of the Honorable Rufus King, of New York, and his mother Sarah Worthington, daughter of Governor Worthington, of Ohio. From such an ancestry flowed many advantages of heredity and example. The solid, practical virtues of a puritan ancestry on the one side, and the chivalric graces and high tone of the Virginia cavalier on the other side, blended by the frankness and enthusiasm of the broader, freer

West—Rufus King was placed at thirteen years of age at Kenyon College, but was transferred from the junior class of that institution to Harvard University, where he graduated with honor, and, after passing through the Law School, then under the teaching of Judge Story and Professor Greenleaf, he came to Cincinnati in March, 1841, fully prepared to begin the "battle of life." He had been brought up by a mother equal to the great responsibility of training and educating boys, and the principles instilled by this good woman guided his life. Soon after coming to Cincinnati, Mr. King married, and in this step he secured a wife whose loving heart was ready to yield every power of her nature to the advancement of her husband, whom she, with prophetic eye, saw was to be a power among men. Through a long life, it was this wife's privilege to stand at his side and to rejoice in the results of his unceasing work for the good of all around him.

Descended on both sides from an ancestry

identified with the political affairs of the nation, there came to Mr. King by heredity a strong inclination to political life, and the first interests which engaged him in his adopted home were of a political nature, and this received encouragement by his connection for a while, in the absence of the editor, with a leading journal. This was at the age of twenty-six years, and at a time when the name of Henry Clay was the inspiration of every heart of the Whig party. With the graceful manners which were Mr. King's through his whole life, he gained the affection of every one, and he was the young hero—the idol of the old Third Ward—the old "Flat Iron Ward." In the same part of the town, though there have been changes made in numbering the wards, he has continued to live, and from this center his influence went out through the entire city. Many were the inducements for him to develop himself in politics and take this path for his life work, but, with the quick penetration of his fine judgment, he saw that in other paths he could best work for the interests of mankind. His refined tastes made him averse to much that would surround him in politics, and though in many ways this life had a fascination for him, he quickly decided to turn his efforts in other directions. All through his life, inducements were held out to him to enter the political arena. He could have had many high offices in the gift of the people, but his convictions were never moved.

The earliest record of Mr. King's public work was in 1846, when he was elected as delegate to the city convention, held May 25th, to form the city charter. In 1848, he was elected councilman from the Third Ward. He served one term. He was there associated with men of mark and influence, for leading citizens fifty years ago were not averse to taking part in municipal affairs. Even at this early age, Mr. King was a leading member of the city council.

Mr. King soon became interested in the public schools, and determined to give his time and work to the development of the system which had already been fully established for many years when he became a member of the school board. He was elected as school visitor from the Third Ward in the year 1851 for the term of two years. He was re-elected each term until the final one in which he served, in 1865, thus making his time of active service in the interests of the public schools fourteen years.

With youth and vigor and enthusiasm, himself a highly educated man, with principles of morality and religion so firmly planted as to seem a part of his nature, he entered upon his work. His personal supervision of the schools, the friendly aid he gave to teachers, for years assisted in making the public schools of Cincinnati models throughout the country.

The point which first attracted Mr. King was the want of proper training in morals and manners—the more complete education of the entire man. It is gratifying to read in the last report (1890) of the superintendent of schools,

Mr. W. H. Morgan, that this point now, after the lapse of so many years, is not neglected— "history, reading, geography, arithmetic, grammar, composition, morals and manners, and German, have been the studies taught." Mr. King's own fine manners, his kindly words, his frequent advice and encouragement, were an education to all who came under his influence. His magnetism was wonderful—it escaped through his eye, through his voice, and every gesture. Mr. King was elected president of the school board in 1852, and was reelected each succeeding year, until he withdrew from the board in 1867.

It is not too much to say that there has never lived in Cincinnati any one who has worked for the cause of education for so many years so effectually and with such good results as Rufus King. Many noble men have given time and labor, and have accomplished much in carrying out certain views and ideas, but no one has had the wide influence, and gave such an impetus to the public schools as

Mr. King. His learning, his varied accomplishments of mind and manner, would not have made him the man of weight and influence he became in Cincinnati, the one who deserved to be called "Cincinnati's most valuable citizen," but he had laid the foundations deep in the hearts of the children while he was yet a young man. Before his thirty years had rolled round, he was known by all the children in all the schools. In this way, if it had been in no other direction, he has been through all the years a marked and invigorating influence in the development of Cincinnati. Stirling principles were implanted through his influence which guided and still guide a large number of those men who have proved themselves Cincinnati's best citizens, and whose love and admiration have followed Mr. King through life. Much of the deep sorrow which pervaded the community when Mr. King passed from hence came from men and women who as children were in these schools.

It is impossible to estimate the wonderful

power Mr. King exercised over the young, and the frequent addresses made before the children in the public schools, in which all the beauty of truth and honesty was set forth, must have sunk deep in those child hearts as they listened to the musical and deep tones of an exceptionally rich voice, coming from a speaker whose whole expression of language and manner was that of the true gentleman.

For many years the young people of Cincinnati had this model before them.

In all these years, Mr. King was steadily occupied in the practice of the law with a vigor and enthusiasm which soon placed him among the leaders in his profession. The very knowledge of the law and his learning gave him greater power in every direction. His capacity for work was wonderful—for forty years not an enterprise connected with the welfare of Cincinnati where his name is not seen among the foremost. Even during those early years, whilst with all his young energy he was laying the foundations of his future sufficient fortune, his purse was open to every need, individual and public, and he had always time to work in other interests than his own.

He gave with a liberality which might have shamed many a millionaire; and here a lesson may be learned by the young just setting out in life—that a stream of generosity may steadily flow without impairing the success of the beneficent individual. It is self-indulgence which causes failure.

Mr. King did not often leave home. He indulged himself in travel at long intervals and for short periods, never long enough to lose his hold upon the affection of his friends nor his own interest in the public welfare. He loved his home and the duties of home-life. He was thoroughly identified with Cincinnati—informing himself in public affairs in every direction, and working for the interests of the community with vigor and intelligence. Who could be better fitted to influence and to lead?

Mr. King's idea of the influence and importance of religious and moral training in the schools may best be known from his own words, taken from his argument in the "Bible Case," which came before the courts in 1869. The question took this name, but it was really an attack upon the entire system of religious and moral training.

The custom of opening the schools with the reading of a portion of Scripture had existed from the very foundation of the schools, and Mr. King regarded it as the most proper and effectual way of bringing the children under control, and of instilling into their minds a reverence for the truest source of all proper training of the human heart—to use his own words, "the eternal, immutable, and essential principles of the Bible—the religion taught by the great Head of all religion."

In 1842, the first complaint came from Bishop Purcell that the Protestant version of the Scriptures was used. Concessions, however, were made, which were satisfactory, and no further trouble came until the outburst which culminated in 1869 to suppress the long-established custom. In November, 1869, the board of education passed the following resolution: "That religious instruction and the reading of religious books, including the Holy Bible, are prohibited in the common schools of Cincinnati, it being the true object and intent of the rule to allow the children of the parents of all sects and opinions in matters of faith and worship to enjoy alike the benefits of the common school fund." Second, that the regulation ordering the "opening exercise in every department shall commence by reading a portion of the Bible by or under the direction of the teachers, and appropriate singing of the pupils," be repealed. Mr. King had resigned from the board of education in 1867, but had never lost his interest in the welfare of the schools. He was retained by those who opposed the action of the board of education. He willingly and earnestly gave himself to what he considered of the most vital importance to the continued success of public school instruction. This effort to banish the Bible from the schools Mr. King opposed in an eloquent and powerful argument.

The following extracts are taken from this argument:

"Why are religion and morality as well as knowledge essential to government? Why was it that the fathers held to that sentiment? Because there were but two principles of power in the government. The one is the virtue of the people, the power of self-government, which gets all its vitality from the Bible; the other is the power of the bayonet; and you can not govern a nation upon any but one of those two principles. For I say in general terms that the nation which throws away the culture and support of religious principle throws away the only enduring security of self-government for the masses, and must come in no great lapse of time to force. It is one thing for scholars and philosophers, sitting in their closets, to refine about this matter—

their fine-spun sentiments may do to govern Utopias, but to govern states is another thing. I speak and your honors are to judge of history, of man in the mass and in action, of the forces essential to guide and control nations, not in sunshine and prosperity only, but when storms run high and the state is distracted and rent by the conflict of men maddened with passion or interest. It is then that safety calls for stronger forces than philosophy or intellect. It must be the deep, eternal forces which curb and compel the most trying emergencies, and which belong only to religious education and faith. "Through the public school, the commonwealth easily and powerfully spreads the tenets of political religion, as Rousseau denominates it, and which he defines in a manner clearly adapted to our constitution and wants. There must be a religious element in public education, or it utterly fails to supply the want. Religion affords security to government, because it holds men, not by the uncertain allegiance of present interest or expediency only, but adds the constant, ever enduring power of the 'still, small voice,' which controls the will and subdues the passions. Secularized religion will not do it. No nation ever obtained even civilization, much less security and happiness, upon the mere light of reason or the laws of nature, unaided by a religious faith. Even pagan rulers courted their priesthood and consulted their oracles. But what is it we want, your honors? It is character, sterling public sentiment, the habit, the enduring universal habit, of resisting wrong and evil, and, among others, let me instance that which seems to be the consuming passion of the American heart, but which the Bible teaches us is the 'root of all evil'—the love of money. Our people, with a servility to wealth which is unaccountable in a truly republican nation, bow down to worship it as blindly as the Israelites did 'the golden calf.' Hence, the frauds and the huge defalcations, the 'rings' and the corruptions, we hear of every day. A man just from the penitentiary, the forger of millions, is followed by a maudlin sympathy, as though a martyr in some great work, and that, too, by the public press. These things do not speak well for us, your honors, and the school board, instead of 'putting down the brakes' upon the moral force of the schools, had better endeavor, by all possible helps, to increase it. I beg leave to inquire what has turned up in the City of Cincinnati, what new dispensation all at once, that encourages these gentlemen to resolve, and say it is time to throw away those aids and restraints which our laws and all experience declare are essential to Society?"

The Woodward and Hughes High Schools were established from endowments, the one by William Woodward, the other by Thomas Hughes. In 1851, these two funds were consolidated and put under the control of a board of managers, consisting of five delegates from the common schools, five from the Woodward board, and two from the Hughes, called the union board. Mr. King was elected president of this board in 1853, which position he continued to hold till the close of his work in this life. In that board, as well as in the district schools, an earnest, efficient coadjutor of Mr. King was Mr. William Hooper, a friend who loved and admired him, and whose friendship was steadfast to the close. He knew and appreciated Mr. King's work. Through all the years that Mr. King was presiding officer of the union board, Mr. Hooper was treasurer. He is now his successor as president.

When the high schools were fully established and in operation, it became necessary to add to the district school system an advanced grade which would fit the pupils for admission into the high schools, and three years after the consolidation of the high school funds and the forming of the union board, the intermediate schools were introduced. Mr. King was one of those most active in putting these schools into operation, and gave both thought and work as trustee and visitor. The school on Ellen street was under the special charge of Mr. King and Mr. William Schultz, in all school affairs his efficient co-worker. This school was a model both in scholarship and order, and for a while Mr. King gave there his most concentrated work. After he was elected president of the school board, his interest became more general and his influence was felt through all the schools of the city.

Mr. King strongly advocated the introduction of vocal music in the schools, and it was mainly through his influence that music attained so high a degree of cultivation under Mr. Aiken in the high schools and Mr. Mason in the district schools. At one time the choral music of the schools in concerts and exhibitions was enjoyed by lovers and students of music, as well as by the young choristers. Mr. King used every influence to encourage the cultivation of music, which he regarded as one of the most powerful aids in humanizing and refining the moral nature of the young.

Normal schools, the Cincinnati University, and city library next interested Mr. King, and in the foundation of each he exerted himself zealously and with success.

In 1859, Mr. King was elected by the city council director of the McMicken University. December 30th of this year, he was elected president of the board of directors for one year, and was re-elected each succeeding year until the year 1870, when the name of the university was changed to "University of Cincinnati," to which he was appointed a director, and again elected president of the board of directors January 2, 1871, and was re-elected each succeeding year until the meeting in January, 1877, when he declined the nomination. Upon that occasion, the board adopted the following resolution: "Resolved, that the thanks of this board are eminently due and are hereby respectfully tendered our retiring chairman, the Honorable Rufus King, for his faithful and energetic labors as chairman of this board, and that this board expresses its sincere regrets that he will no longer continue to exercise the functions which he has for the last six years administered with such fidelity, urbanity, and impartiality."

To the University of Cincinnati in its early years, perhaps, was given more of Mr. King's time and thoughtful, earnest work than any other interest outside of his profession—here, indeed, his legal knowledge was often needed, and was cheerfully and gratuitously given.

So many active, intelligent, and able men were giving their energetic work to the development of the McMicken fund for establishing a university that it might seem unjust to select Mr. King as foremost in the work, but facts will tell more than words of how much is due to him.

For years after the death of Mr. McMicken, which occurred but a short time before the breaking out of the civil war, property fell in value, and much of the property left by Mr.

McMicken was in the southern portion of the United States. The Cincinnati property was in a dilapidated condition, and no fixed income could be depended upon. Not only business talent, but legal knowledge and good judgment were needed. That Mr. King was made president of the board of directors shows in what esteem he was held. His reports during these dark years, given over his own name, show the prudence, the judgment, the wisdom, with which every thing was managed, and it was not until a sure income was provided, by rebuilding, improving, etc., that educational work was begun.

Another fact showing how pre-eminent Mr. King was in carrying out wisely Mr. McMicken's plans was the aid he gave his noble mother in all her work in the development of the McMicken School of Design. Mr. McMicken had founded this school by a gift of one thousand dollars to purchase casts of antique statuary for the use of such a school. At that time it was not connected with the university, but it kept alive in the hearts of the people by its efficient work the greater work to come. For years, this little school stood as a reminder of the beneficent founder, and gave courage to carry out the greater design.

Mr. King's work in the public interests was, as are the silent forces of nature, quiet and unobtrusive. He was singularly modest, and when the results of effort came, though it might bring down the admiration of the whole community, he cared not for any recognition of the part he had borne. He loved to work in the background and to put others forward for the glory of achievement.

His good judgment, his legal knowledge, helped to lay the foundations in many directions of the public good that Cincinnati now enjoys. An illustration of this is seen in the grand library which is Cincinnati's pride.

When Mr. King became a member of the board of education, each district school received an appropriation from the tax fund for the formation of a library. These libraries were insignificant, necessarily. The books were constantly duplicated. One library illustrated all the others. To Mr. King first came the idea of uniting these small streams into the full and generous flow, and he found earnest and able support in his associates, who were men well fitted to lay the foundation of a library for public use. Mr. King's opinions and plans were always treated with marked respect, so that he might justly be regarded as the foremost builder of our great and useful library. This at the time was accorded to him, and, without doubt, there was not a man in Cincinnati who united so many necessary talents to carry out this suggestion as Mr. King. For the accomplishment of this end, it was necessary the law should be changed. Mr. King drew up the new law, going to Columbus and working in every way to carry it through. There was opposition, as in all such enterprises, but the influence was overwhelming and the new law was passed.

A board of directors was appointed, and

Mr. King was elected in 1867 a member of this board. At a meeting held May 14, 1870, he was elected president of the library board by the votes of his fellow-members, Messrs. Henry Probasco, Dr. William B. Davis, William Tilden, Robert Brown, Herman Eckel, and Francis Ferry. The combined appropriations were sufficient to warrant the directors in laying the foundations on a broad scale. These gentlemen were men of intelligence and cultivation, and, with a man of scholarly attainments and wide knowledge of books as their president, whose influence was felt and whose opinions were always regarded, many rare and useful books were brought together. An excellent plan was adopted in soliciting lists from specialists, who were urged to put down valuable works in science and art as books of reference, and which none but the wealthy could obtain for private libraries.

It may not be generally known, but books of exceeding value can be found in the scientific and art departments of the public library.

Mr. King continued to act as presiding officer of the board until 1873. On June 30th of this year, he resigned from the board of management. Mr. King felt that the first great object was accomplished, and he wished to give time and labor in other more urgent ways. Because of this limitation put upon his work in his own good judgment, he was enabled to aid in many more directions than he could have done had he indulged himself in the enjoyment of well-arranged work already prepared and systematized. Though in many instances Mr. King will be found working with undiminished energy in the same direction, yet his great talent was as an organizer, and his character was peculiarly adapted to the complication and difficulties attending the first steps of an enterprise.

Mr. William F. Poole, librarian of the library in Boston, was elected October 26, 1869, and accepted the position of librarian of the Cincinnati Library, November 15th of the same year, and served until '1874. Mr. Poole was known to be a man of great ability in arranging and cataloguing books—acknowledged on all sides to be the foremost man in the country in his profession. He left the library in excellent condition when he went to Chicago to take charge of the great library there. One of the most able of the co-workers of Mr. King in all educational affairs was Mr. Charles P. James, for a number of years past judge of the Supreme Court of the District of Columbia. Judge James expresses himself in a letter so justly and with such true appreciation of Mr. King's first work in the library, that his own words should be read. No testimony could be more reliable, for Mr. King and Judge James worked side by side for the public interest, long, earnestly, and manfully.

"I have tried to recall Mr. King's long devotion to the school children of Cincinnati, but at last the great fact makes only a strong picture with only a few strong details. I remember well the admiration with which I chiefly looked on while he accomplished results. I recall the economy of time which enabled him without interrupting his busy practice to inspect the work of a school on his way to and from court; how he managed to find time for committee meetings; how he suggested methods to teachers; how he drew up as a lawyer even the contracts for school-houses, and by his firmness compelled evasive contractors to keep their bargains honestly; and especially how he made arrangements with the county treasurer for an advance of school funds before all his accounts were settled. In a word, while he had from many persons faithful co-operation, it always seemed to me it was his hand that planned and guided. When the legislature revised the tax for the purchase of libraries, it was, I think, under Mr. King's lead that the funds for all the districts of Cincinnati were consolidated. At the beginning, we spent all our money for books and had none left for shelving. My impression is that it was Mr. King who arranged a school children's concert in Pike's Opera House, where nine hundred young voices drew together a dense crowd of mothers and fathers, and so built the alcoves for the first nucleus of the consolidated 'Public School Library.' I should be careful not to exclude coadjutors, but my clear impression at the time, as I sat with 'authorities' in a stage box, was that even such a detail as that concert had been either suggested or guided by Mr. King. I recall that it was a common opinion that he was rendering for many years a kind of service (gratuitously) for which an official expects high compensation, and that he never 'got tired.' Perhaps one of the most definite impressions of these days was his unfailing patience at the Monday night board meetings. I fancy that oratory was as distasteful to him as it was to me, but the orators never saw any impatience on his face.

"It is more than thirty years since all these things happened. Perhaps, after all, the impression that a man makes on his associates is as strong a testimony to his deeds and their value as recorded details would be.

"I am glad you intend to preserve the memory of so much usefulness and such fidelity. It is of public importance. It should not be lost."

Mr. King was elected a member of the convention called in 1874 to amend the state constitution. The place of meeting was Columbus, and the delegates assembled in May and chose as their president the Honorable Morrison R. Waite, of Toledo. In October they adjourned to Cincinnati, and soon after Mr. Waite received the appointment of chief justice of the United States, and Mr. King was elected to fill his place as president of the convention.

Already had Mr. King made the acquaintance of every member of the convention, and as their presiding officer was honored and admired. His home was the center of a generous and gracious hospitality extended to every member of the convention. For four or five months, there were social gatherings of every kind at his house—breakfast parties, dinner parties, and evening receptions—not a single member of the convention who did not enjoy Mr. King's warm hospitalities, and from every part of the state have come repeated recognitions of kindness received.

No individual act can give to a community a more important character abroad than hospitality to strangers. Perhaps no one in Cincinnati has done more in this way than Mr. King. His house was always noted for its ever-flowing, generous, unostentatious hospitality, and there never was an opportunity of showing it more fully than on an occasion which drew together representative men from every part of the state. It was not only on this occasion, but on all occasions of the coming together of strangers was Mr. King foremost in kindly attentions. Party politics did not affect his gentlemanlike, genial course. A few such men have a wonderful influence in giving tone and reputation to a city. Throughout the country was Mr. Rufus King's name gratefully remembered in connection with the many charming attractions of Cincinnati. The simplicity of Mr. King's taste pervaded all he did. With ample means to live in ostentation and display, his entertainments never exceeded generous, tasteful simplicity.

Mr. King's abilities as a public speaker were very marked, and until late in life he was sought for on every occasion of public demonstration where eloquence was needed to plead before the crowded audience, or where grace and suavity were required at the dinner table. An inspiration always accompanied his presence, and a flow of gladness was the result.

All this work for education and for the public interest generally was outside of the chief occupation of Mr. King's life, which was to carry out in all its grand possibilities the profession he had chosen for his life work.

His ideas of the law were broad and comprehensive. He did not use it merely as a means of gain. The eternal principles of truth and honesty, of justice, he wished to establish. His own fine character owed much of its harmony, its calmness, to the training of the law. He might be regarded as an illustration of what that noble study may develop.

No men have it in their power to stamp the character of a community in every direction so decidedly as men of the legal profession. They are brought in contact in many more ways, and more vitally, with their fellow-men, than any other class, and, by an upright, honest, manly course, can instil ideas of honor and truth which others have not the opportunity to do.

Among the foremost of those men true to their noble profession was Rufus King. For forty years he was president of the Bar Association of Cincinnati, and it is only necessary to call attention to the large meeting convened on the occasion of the death of Mr. King, to see how he was held in the hearts of all his brothers in the profession he loved so well. All over the state he was known and appreciated. No one at the bar had a higher place than Mr. King. When these words came from one of Ohio's leading lawyers, it seemed to be the voice of the whole profession:

"I looked upon him as one of the finest characters of the state—of great intellect, of taintless honesty, a heart as tender as a child, a disposition mild as a summer's breeze."

This disposition always attracted the young to him, and his influence over young men was one of the most remarkable and beneficent features of his life.

Mr. King's connection with the Cincinnati Law School, which began in the year 1875, continued until his death. He was appointed dean of the faculty, and for a few years held this place; but finding the position required more time and labor than he could give with justice to his work in other directions, he resigned the deanship, but continued to lecture on constitutional law and the law of real property. These subjects were of especial interest to him, and his ideas had been matured by long study and reflection. This part of his legal work gave him great pleasure in the closing years of his life here. He had all the qualities of mind and character necessary to make a great lawyer. Through years of devotion to his profession, he had learned to love the law, and to teach it, in its noblest, broadest meaning, was to him a duty, and, therefore, a happiness. This pleasure was increased by the fact that he was helping to carry on a work his father had begun.

The Cincinnati Law School was founded in 1833 by Judge John C. Wright, Mr. Edward King, and Mr. Timothy Walker, afterward Judge Walker. It was the first institution for legal instruction established in the West. In 1835, the school was connected with the Cincinnati College, and, under its auspices, was revived. Mr. King's teaching in the Law School was not confined to the routine lecture, but he was ready to explain and to go over difficult points, and never seemed wearied. He could always be found after his lecture surrounded by an admiring and eager group, who were taking in the benign influence of his sunny nature.

He always saw the sunny side of life, and this made him the beloved friend of the young. It was a great pleasure to Mr. King to extend his hospitalities to the law students, especially those who were strangers in the city, and on occasions of Thanksgiving, Christmas, etc., it was his delight to gather around his dinner table those who were away from home and friends. Mr. King never was more happy than when he was contributing to the pleasure of others. His conversation sparkled with wit and anecdote, and no doubt this little reminder would bring from many distant points happy recollections of these occasions. It was often remarked by those in daily intercourse with Mr. King, both at home and at his office, that he was never despondent; his words were always hopeful and full of encouragement. Life seemed to him always serene and unclouded—at least, he could always discern behind the clouds the blessed source of light and life. This, combined with the earnestness and dignity of his character, made his life truly a " gospel of glad tidings."

The Cincinnati Law Library Association was organized on June 5, 1847. The gentlemen present on this occasion were Messrs. Rufus King, Charles Anderson, Alphonso Taft, Bellamy Storer, Salmon P. Chase, and a number of other lawyers. Twice in the history of this library has fire interrupted its progress. In 1849, the court-house was destroyed by fire, and nothing of consequence was done by the library association until June 7, 1851, when the board met and again organized.

On this occasion, Mr. King was elected vice-president. In 1855, he was elected president, and filled that office until his death, a period of thirty-six years. There was nothing connected with Mr. King's profession which interested him more and commanded more of his time and thought than this library. He looked upon it as the source of enlightenment and learning for the legal profession in Cincinnati. He gave freely of his time and money, and on the occasion of the destruction of the books by fire in 1884, when the courthouse with its valuable contents was also destroyed, Mr. King came forward and paid off the indebtedness of the library, which amounted to $3,885. It was this act of liberality on the part of Mr. King, and his unceasing efforts to arouse the bar of Cincinnati to the importance of the work, which caused the re-establishment of the library, resulting in eminent success. Mr. King's interest has not passed away with the close of his mortal life. He left twenty thousand dollars for the benefit of the library to which he had given so much of his best thought and work.

As a young lawyer, Mr. King impressed himself as few young men do. He was not twenty-six years of age when the attorneyship of a leading bank was offered him. High standing and influential friends suggested the idea, but the suggestion was taken up, encouraged, and determined by the president of the Commercial Bank, Judge James Hall, a man of known ability and judgment, who recognized Mr. Rufus King's talents and power and urged his appointment. This was an opportunity and a beginning which is rarely the good fortune of a young lawyer, and was an introduction which brought a constantly increasing and soon lucrative practice.

Such was Mr. King's popularity, and so great was the confidence placed in his judgment, that he was sought and consulted in every enterprise which has developed the interests of Cincinnati. He was a many-sided man, and a man who informed himself well in every direction, and his work was efficient wherever it was given.

At an early period of his life, he saw the need of a railroad communication with the South, and long before the Southern Railroad was built, his eloquent tongue was pleading for its existence. He took part in the early development of the road, actively and efficiently, as its history will show. For a while, he was forced to accept its presidency, but he felt that work in this direction should be all-absorbing, and for this he was not prepared. Neither the proper training nor his tastes inclined him to take up this work further than to give his influence and his financial aid, so far as was in his power. Mr. King was also at one time vice-president of the Hamilton and Dayton road, and for about a year acting president, during the illness of Mr. Shoemaker, the president.

"It would be difficult to keep all trace of Mr. King as an active participant in the popular public service of the best citizens of Cincinnati, for its highest and most permanent good. Of late years, his most important and valuable services to the city were rendered as a member of the tax commission, of which he was one of the original members, and whose term would have expired in May of 1891 had not the so-called charter bill dispensed with that board. Mr. King was looked upon as its wisest adviser, as the member best informed not only on municipal affairs, but also in the details as managed or mismanaged under the law. In all these concerns, he showed a keen insight and broad comprehension. No principle was overlooked, no detail escaped his attention in the work, apportioning to each of city funds the money to which it was entitled from the tax levy for city salaries and expenses.

"Against false or dubious claims, exorbitant estimates, and all insidious 'incidentals,' as the official 'pickings and stealings' were called, he always stood as the rock of Gibralter, and it was just by such sturdy resistance, always aided by his fellow-members of the board, that it came to be regarded by the board of the sinking fund as the safeguard of the city finances." The board of tax commissioners was created by the act of the legislature passed April 16, 1883, and was organized on the 14th of the May following. It consisted of three freeholders, appointed by the

Superior Court, the mayor, and the city comptroller. Mr. King was appointed for the full term of three years, Mr. Henry Urner for two years, and Mr. Larz Anderson for one year. The mayor was president *ex-officio*. Mr. King was elected vice-president, and the records show that the duties of chairmanship were more frequently performed by him than by the president. Mr. King was reappointed by the court for a second term, and was again elected vice-president, and continued to serve until the board was abolished by the legislature in 1891. Mr. King attended the final meeting of the board.

The Committee of One Hundred was organized by public opinion in October of 1885, preceding the fall elections, and was composed of leading men and property holders. Mr. King was one of the original members, and as such served on its most important committees, such as election, police, etc. In this service, he gave much time and advice in the preparation of the registration and election laws, especially the latter. The active work was performed through the first three or four years. Mr. King's membership was maintained until the dissolution of the committee in 1891.

When one regards Mr. King as a lawyer, fully prepared for all the hard work of his profession, faithfully performing every obligation of a large practice, gaining a place among the highest, one marvels that time could have been found for work in any other direction; but so great, so varied, was this outside work, that it becomes almost an impossibility to gather up its records. The results are seen every-where, and from the great channels of work flow lesser streams, enriching and refreshing places unseen and unnoticed. This is especially applicable to Mr. King's charitable work. He often made large gifts which called forth the praise of all, but the daily flow of his charities—the open hand, the kindly smile, the hopeful words—this is known only to the grateful hearts that he blest, and to One who rewards the "cheerful giver."

Mr. King's charities flowed not only from a generous heart, but from a just heart. It was a firm principle with him that to give was a duty. Freely he gave of his abundance, and with material aid always went out the encouraging word, the kindly smile.

Mr. King's legal counsel was given gratuitously to many charitable institutions, and both Catholic and Protestant acknowledged it with gratitude. He remembered the poor, he remembered the church, he remembered the profession he loved so well, in the last disposition he made of his property.

The benefits of his charitable heart were bestowed through his life and will still continue to bless.

The beauty and excellence of Mr. King's character were shown in all his intentions—the wisdom and greatness of his intellect in the way these intentions were carried out. Bravely and firmly he defended the right, which he believed with all his heart would at last prevail.

In every art enterprise which has grown up in Cincinnati in the last fifty years, the name of Rufus King will be found among the foremost and most energetic supporters. The College of Music, which has done and is doing so much for the musical fame of Cincinnati, and which owes its direct foundation to the fine administrative talent and ability and devotion of Colonel George Ward Nichols and the munificent generosity of Mr. Reuben Springer, had an inspiration and vital encouragement from Mr. King, which is feelingly acknowledged by the trustees of the College of Music in a beautiful tribute made a short time after Mr. King's death, in which they speak of him as "one of the founders and most devoted friends." Colonel Nichols had a warm friendship for Mr. King, and talked with him freely on all his plans, and respected his judgment. All know that encouragement coming from a respected source often brings to maturity ideas which without it would never be expressed. At Mr. King's dinner table was first discussed the plan of bringing Mr. Theodore Thomas to Cincinnati as head of the College of Music and permanent leader of the festivals. Mr. King urged upon Colonel Nichols prompt action, and the same evening he set forth for New York to consult with Mr. Thomas.

In all the early work which resulted in the establishment of the Art Museum, Mr. King interested himself with great vigor. Step by step did the crowning ornament of Cincinnati advance. The story of its rise has been told and is known to every one. In all the early records of work done in this direction, Mr. King's name will be found among the most efficient and valuable workers.

Had Mr. King's life been prolonged for a few years more, it is probable that his pen would have been active in giving out from his great accumulation of knowledge much that would have added to the literary fame of Cincinnati. He had in contemplation to make his last years here useful in this way. Among other things, it was his wish to enlarge his history of Ohio, which he had written under the disadvantage of being compelled to abridge the volume to a uniform size of a series for which he had undertaken to write. As it is, the book is wonderfully complete, and could only have been written by a man of great historical research, with a legal and statesmanlike turn of mind. Mr. King's great desire, however, was to prepare a much-needed law book on a subject which for years had been a study of deep thought and research. That this work could not have been finished must always be regretted.

Mr. King was elected a director of Spring Grove Cemetery in 1878. He interested himself zealously in the improvements of this beautiful city of rest. Here, as elsewhere, his legal advice was of great value. His fellow-workers in the board of directors testify most feelingly to his able and efficient work. The last meeting for public work Mr. King attended was on the 5th of February, when he met for the last time the board of directors of Spring Grove Cemetery.

Mr. King always manifested an active interest in religious movements in every direction. The church which seemed to meet his own requirements best was the Protestant Episcopal Church, and he was a constant attendant for many years of St. Paul's Church, and was an active vestryman for thirty-six consecutive years. From this center he worked, but he did not confine his aid nor interest to this parish. His liberality was well understood and was generally felt. His purse was always open to the needs of the church. His contributions were large, and on one occasion he relieved St. Paul's Church of a debt of over three thousand dollars, reserving to himself the compensation of being allowed to secure an endowment fund for the church by such legal forms as to make the interest of the fund only available for use. The gratitude of generations to come will surely be his, for the wisdom, the foresight, the generosity, which led him to secure a fund always sufficient for the maintenance of at least a mission church in the heart of Cincinnati. Mr. King was active in both diocesan and parish work. He was always the personal friend and legal adviser of Bishop McIlvaine, and also of Bishop Bedell. During the short period of Bishop Jaggar's active work, Mr. King was his close friend and adviser, and it is only necessary to read the beautiful tribute of Bishop Vincent at the last diocesan convention, to see the high esteem in which he held Mr. King, and how he would have valued the wise counsels and efficient aid of such a layman.

In all the affairs of Kenyon College, Mr. King was a faithful and energetic trustee. Especially did he uphold the interests of the theological department, and for many years he gave time, thought, and money to this work. It can best be seen how Mr. King was regarded as a churchman by repeating the words of Bishop Vincent:

"One of the greatest shocks on my recent return to the diocese was the news of the irreparable loss it had sustained in the death of Mr. King. I regret exceedingly that my own short residence among you leaves me ignorant of Mr. King's early life and prevents my giving it that notice here which I would like to, but it was a life which in its influence and results was known to the whole community. His chosen profession of the law knew him as one of its leading lights; the world of letters recognized him as a scholar and historian; the city and state proudly pointed to him as a representative citizen. His personal and social qualities attracted the admiration and the love of all who knew him. His influence in the home life and in the family circle was ideal—to us, though, he seems most conspicuous as a high-minded Christian layman. It was his Christian uprightness and devout faith, his love of his church, his steady and generous devotion to her good, which shed the finest luster over his life. Although he never sat, I believe, in any of her public councils, he had, nevertheless, as trustee of the diocese and of our Gambier institutions, been for many years one of the church's most trusted counsellors, always alive not merely to her legal and financial interest, but to her highest spiritual welfare also. The last indisputable proof of this he gave in the provisions of his will, in which, after many other charitable bequests, he crowned them all by the munificent gifts of $1,000 to our Diocesan Children's Hospital and $50,000 to the trustees of the diocese for the maintenance of two or more itinerant missionaries. His sagacious mind saw the most important interest and sorest need of this church of ours to-day, and his generous heart and hand provided for it. Let us thank God, as the generations to come will thank Him, for this noble layman."

Simply as an outline of a noble life, has this little sketch been written—only to bring together in a compact form the various outlets of a benevolent heart. All this benevolence was guided by a mind and character perfectly trained. Cool judgment, firm principles, directed every impulse which came from his great heart.

Mr. King's life, written out with all its elaborate work, would fill volumes, and at last could only tell what may be said in a few words—that Rufus King worked with wisdom, with enthusiasm, with devotion, with no thought of self, for the best interests of his fellow-men. The good influence of such a life reaches out indefinitely, and its practical results can not be calculated.

The whole of Mr. King's life is a testimony to the expanding, ennobling influence of a perfect trust in the wisdom and love of God, and confidence in the future higher and truer life.

In no way has the example of this good man been a greater help than in showing how noble and beneficent a life may be led by following strictly the teachings of our Savior, Christ, and making our lives, as was His, full of works of love and mercy.

Rufus King's work in this world is finished. He has passed from among men. Trustfully and peacefully he closed his eyes on earthly scenes, and has entered his eternal home.

He died on the 25th of March, 1891.

SUMMARY

OF THE

VARIOUS WORKS IN WHICH MR. KING DEVOTED TIME AND LABOR FOR THE PUBLIC INTERESTS.

1846—Delegate to form city charter.

1848—Councilman.

1851—School visitor; member of the union
1865 board of high schools; member board
1867 of education; member of the board of
1870 managers of the public library, and
1873 library board; president of each.

1859—Director of the university from the start
1877 to close of second term, appointed.

1883—Tax commissioner, twice appointed by
1891 Superior Court.

1885—Member of the committee of one hun-
1891 dred, created by public opinion.

In addition to this, Mr. King filled at various

times, and for a number of years each, the following positions:

Dean of the Cincinnati Law School.
President of the Law Library Association.
President of the Cincinnati Bar Association.
Trustee of the Southern Diocese of Ohio.
Trustee of Kenyon College.
Vestryman of St. Paul's Church.
Director of Spring Grove Cemetery.
Vice-president and committeeman of the American Bar Association.
Vice-president for Ohio of the Social Science Association.
Director of Southern R. R., Hamilton and Dayton R. R., C. H. & I. R. R., etc.

APPENDIX.

FUNERAL SERVICES AT ST. PAUL'S CHURCH.

MARCH 28, 1891.

A very large assemblage was present at St. Paul's Church to assist at the funeral services of the late Honorable Rufus King, which were of a deeply impressive character. Mr. King had been connected with St. Paul's Church for more than fifty years, and was always deeply interested in its welfare. The somber hangings which veiled altar and chancel on Good Friday were still in place, and gave additional solemnity to the scene.

The procession was met at the church porch by the Rev. Dr. Benedict, rector of St. Paul's; Rev. Dr. Pise, rector of Christ Church, Glendale; Rev. Dr. Tinsley, rector of the Church of the Advent, and the full vested choir of

St. Paul's—fifty men and boys—the solemn tramp of the men unbroken by any music of voice or organ. Returning to the chancel, Rev. Dr. Benedict, leading the way, recited the opening sentences of the service which the Prayer Book calls "The Order for the Burial of the Dead," beginning, "I am the Resurrection and the Life, whoever liveth and believeth in Me shall never die."

The great anthem, "Lord, let me know my end and the number of my days," was chanted with deep impressiveness by a quartet of men's voices—Mr. David Davis, Mr. Ashe, Mr. Tyrrell, and Dr. Tate. Rev. Dr. Tinsley read the lesson, "Now is Christ risen from the dead," and Dr. Benedict recited the concluding prayers, the responses being rendered with deep feeling by the congregation.

The choral part of the service was very beautiful. Hymn 91, "It is not death to die," had been selected, and the Retrocessional was the triumphant Alleluia, the voices of the choristers rising to a glorious burst of melody at the verse:

> "But lo! there breaks a yet more glorious day;
> The saints triumphant rise in bright array;
> The King of Glory passes on his way.
> Alleluia!"

And dying to the mutest whisper as the procession reached to the vestry-room.

The interment was at Spring Grove.

The pall-bearers were selected from the many public bodies with which Mr. King had been associated, and were as follows:

Tax Commission—T. H. C. Allen, J. B. Mosby.

Cemetery Association—Robt. Hosea, Henry Probasco.

Trustees of the Diocese of Southern Ohio—Larz Anderson, Charles W. Short.

Law Library—Judge Harmon, M. W. Myers.

Bar of Hamilton County—W. L. Avery, M. F. Force, W. S. Groesbeck, J. W. Herron, Lawrence Maxwell.

Law School Faculty—J. D. Cox, G. R. Sage.

Law School Students—T. H. Darby, E. G. Kincaid.

University of Cincinnati—C. G. Comegys, W. M. Ramsey.

Cincinnati College—M. B. Hagans, W. H. Neff.

Historical and Philosophical Society of Ohio E. F. Bliss, F. J. Jones.

Harvard Club—George Hoadly, Jr., Julius Dexter.

Library—William Rendigs, A. W. Whelpley.

And S. J. Thompson, Channing Richards, and R. P. Ernst, Mr. King's partners.

MEMORIAL MEETING OF THE CINCINNATI BAR

IN THE U. S. COURT-ROOM.

[*From the Cincinnati Commercial Gazette.*]

The large U. S. Court-room in the Government Building was closely filled yesterday during the meeting of the bar in memory of the late Rufus King. All the courts of record had adjourned for the day in view of this meeting and the funeral sevices in the afternoon. It was an occasion of memorable interest, as well on account of the high character of the assemblage as that of the departed jurist and noble-spirited citizen whose name was to be called in remembrance.

Hon. Aaron F. Perry was called to the chair by motion of Lawrence Maxwell, Jr., and J. D. Brannan was elected secretary. Mr. Samuel J. Thompson, the law partner of Mr. King, was to have been one of the speakers, but was unable to be present on account of illness. With this exception, and the introduction of a letter from ex-Governor Hoadly, the arrangements for the meeting as published on Friday were carried out. Ex-Judge Force permitted himself the gratification, sad though it was, of coming down from Sandusky to attend.

Two hours were occupied by the speeches, without a sign of weariness in any part of the large gathering. While admiration fulfilling its purpose as a tribute to the dead, the meeting had a value as an inspiration to the living which no one present could have failed to recognize.

The duty of drafting a suitable memorial for adoption by the meeting had been previously assigned to a committee composed entirely of present and former law partners of Mr. King, to wit: Judge Sage, Mr. Samuel J. Thompson, Hon. John W. Herron, Mr. Julius Dexter, ex-Judge Avery, Mr. Lawrence Maxwell, Jr., and Mr. Channing Richards. The memorial was written by Judge Sage, and, like the gem prepared by Judge Harmon as the expression of the Law Library Association, there is much said in a few words.

The memorial was as follows:

Rufus King died on the morning of Wednesday, 25th of March, 1891, at his home on East Third street, in this city where he had lived for more than forty years.

He was born at Chillicothe, Ohio, May 30, 1817. He received his academic education at Kenyon College and at Harvard University. After a full course at the Harvard Law School, under the tuition of Justice Joseph Story and Simon Greenleaf, he came in 1841 to Cincinnati, was admitted to the practice, and starting alone in his profession, was at once retained as counsel by the Commercial Bank, and almost immediately secured a large and lucrative clientage. It was not long before he was recognized as a leader at the bar which numbered among the members Chase and Walker and Spencer and Groesbeck and Storer and

Worthington, and many others of scarcely less prominence. That position he held during the entire period of his active practice, which he continued to hold till about his seventieth year. Devoted as he was to his profession, and ever faithful as he was to the trusts reposed in him by his clients, he nevertheless found time, which the diligent man can always find, to do more than his share toward the advancement of the best interests of the city of his adoption. Rejecting offer after offer of public positions of prominence and profit, he applied himself with his accustomed energy to improving the condition of the common schools of Cincinnati. So generally were his labors in this behalf recognized and appreciated, that not only was he elected and re-elected a member of the board of education time and again, and yet again and again, by the voters of his ward, which was then known as the "Flat Iron Ward," notwithstanding the majority was largely against him politically, but he was also, during almost the entire period of his services, kept at the head of the board as its president. Those were the golden days in the history of the common schools, and Rufus King did more for the upbuilding of that system than any other one man living or dead. To him we are largely indebted for our magnificent public library.

He was one of the founders and constant supporters of our law library. His helping and bounteous hand came to the rescue when that library was destroyed in the turbulent scenes of 1884. He was one of the most honored and distinguished lecturers of the law school of the Cincinnati College. Of more than ordinary literary attainments, he was a great reader of the best authors and a writer of clearness, elegance, and force. His history of Ohio, one of the best of the American Commonwealth Series, published in 1888, was prepared with great pains and labor, and is a valuable and lasting contribution to the annals of the state. So long as he had strength, he was ever ready and willing and anxious to do whatever his hand could find to do to benefit his neighbor, and every man was his neighbor. As a lawyer, he was learned, honorable, diligent, and successful. Always vigilant in the interests of his clients, he never failed to maintain his own integrity and the high standard of the honor of his profession. As a citizen, he was active, independent, unselfish, public-spirited, and efficient; and as a man, pure in life, in thought, and in action. With all his professional and public cares and duties, his love for his home life and his filial devotion for his widowed mother were among the most conspicuous and beautiful traits of his character. Now that he is dead, we may say without reserve every thing that is true of him without saying one thing that is bad of him. This is one of the exceedingly rare occasions when there can be no friction nor clashings between the maxims *nil nisi verum* and *nil nisi bonum*.

The bar, as sincere mourners deploring the loss of one of its oldest, best loved, and most honored members, with heartfelt sympathy for his widow in the loneliness of her bereavement, offer this tribute, imperfect and inadequate though it be, to his memory.

Following the reading of the memorial, Hon. Aaron F. Perry paid from the chair his tribute to the worth of the deceased. Language could hardly convey a more delicate reference than his to the part Mrs. King had in sharing her husband's career:

Mr. Perry's Tribute.

Your honors of the various branches of the judiciary and brethren of the bar—To some of us who have long shared the labors and experiences incident to practical enforcement of justice as defined by jurisprudence, imperfectly it may be, but more perfectly than elsewhere defined by human learning, meetings of this kind follow each other with startling emphasis. We can not if we would, and would not if we could, abstain from manly sorrow, which suffuses the eyes with unbidden moisture and reminds us of valued associations, to be ours never more.

Rufus King, a man of liberal culture, a lawyer of ability and success, passes from our companionship.

It is impracticable to describe or characterize a prolonged professional career, uniform in its general features of honor and success.

In the departure of Rufus King, we can not make the mistake of treating it as an ordinary loss. He was descended on his father's side from a patriotic stock not unknown for its influence in aid of the federal constitution. He was also the son of a mother widely distinguished by philanthropic zeal in charitable and religious movements, not limited to her own country, but which gave her a large welcome and much admiration in distinguished circles elsewhere.

If I might, without lack of delicacy, lift the corner of a mourning veil, I would say that Rufus King was fortunate otherwise than in his parentage. A careful and admirable biography of his distinguished mother was written by the only lady who could have been with her enough to finish so careful a portrait; a work of delicacy and admiration, which may be fairly supposed to disclose the pride and happiness of the artist. No woman not happy in her relations with the son could have so admired the mother.

While Mr. King was a lover of literary acquirements, he seemed to cherish an uncommon aptitude for details in business transactions—for analyzing accounts and testing the accuracy of technical procedure. During many successive years, he has charged himself with the duty of making estimates on several branches of taxation for the city government. His practical interest in the active trial of litigated cases has been diminishing. But he is said to have given much labor and care to his lectures in the law school. I have repeatedly heard his pupils speak of their interest in his lectures and of their exceptional value. Mr.

King was for many years a zealous and punctual member of the Bar Association of Cincinnati; also of the state and United States associations. Whether he discontinued his relations with them, I am not informed. When the last constitutional convention was held in Cincinnati, Morrison R. Waite was its president. Mr. King was one of its most prominent members. When Mr. Waite was made chief-justice of the Supreme Court of the United States, Mr. King was made president of the convention, and served to its close with full satisfaction to the members and to the people of the state at large. I know of no reason which would have made the appointment of Mr. King to be chief-justice less acceptable than the appointment of Mr. Waite. We now know that Mr. Waite was happily adapted to that great office. We only lack knowledge whether Mr. King would have been successful to the same extent that we lacked knowledge whether Mr. Waite would be successful before he was tried.

Hon. Wm. M. Ramsey was the next to address the meeting. He said:

When the life of a great and good man is terminated by death, we are accustomed to say, "his loss is irreparable," "the void can not be filled." These expressions are sometimes criticised and condemned as being mere rhetorical exaggerations. It is said that in the progress of events the death will soon be forgotten, and that no perceptible consequence will follow it; that the world will move right on. The criticism proceeds from misapprehension of the meaning of the expression. It does not mean that another, or many others, the equal of the departed one, may not remain, but it means that the fields in which such men toil are not at any time sufficiently supplied with laborers, that there is more work to be done than men to do it, and that the diminution of ranks already too thin is an irreparable calamity. There are, indeed, patriots and philanthropists surviving Rufus King, but they have more work than they can do.

If all were patriots and philanthropists, the fall of one would be a calamity only to his immediate circle, and not to the state or to society. But some are neither patriots nor philanthropists. Some are teachers by precept or example, or both, of false doctrines. Some are digging at the very foundations of the social fabric. Some are ignorant; some are weak. Some stand neutral in the mighty contest between right and wrong. Hence, the good and the great can not be stricken down without general loss and general lamentation. Rufus King was a thorough American of the highest and best type. His character had evidently been formed upon the models of the revolutionary period of our history. That was a period of heroism and self-sacrifice. It was a period of unselfishness, of patriotism and philanthropy. He listened to the recital of its events from the lips of both father and mother in his childhood. The personal share of his immediate ancestors in its sufferings and achievements caused him to realize its full significance and to imbibe its spirit. The children of revolutionary parents and their children's children received a direct legacy composed of the glory of that period, and it enriched them more than any or all other bequests and devises. Rufus King was educated in sight of Bunker Hill and Lexington.

He was at all times a student and lover of American history. It was from the example of Washington himself that he learned it was good to serve one's country without hire or salary, and he followed that illustrious example. He devoted his time, his energies, his talents, to the public service during his whole life without pecuniary reward. He labored unceasingly in the interests of popular education, because he knew that ignorance is the greatest barrier to human happiness. His idea of a public school was that expressed in the bill of rights in our constitution, to wit, that religion, morality, and knowledge go hand in hand, and that they are " essential to good government." He labored in the cause of reform in municipal government, because he saw in the misgovernment of the cities a deadly menace to the safety and welfare of the people. He was foremost in every effort to promote the interests of the masses of his fellow-men, for his philanthropy was not limited to any class.

I knew Mr. King when he was in active and distinguished practice at the bar. He was the same bright, energetic, attractive, aggressive, and honorable gentleman in that relation that he was in all others. He was cheerful but dignified. He always had something attractive and sparkling to say wholly outside of the commonplace.

One could not come in contact with him without experiencing an agreeable sensation. He was inspiring and inspiriting. He had a tonic influence. It was because he was genuine and true as well as gifted and accomplished. Such a man is not only the subject of admiration, but of affection. Some weeks ago, many members of the bar of Cincinnati met to testify their esteem of one of its distinguished members who had announced his retirement from the duties of his profession. Mr. King had been expected, but was detained at his house by illness. A letter from him explaining and regretting his absence was read. Those of you who were present on that occasion will well remember the reception which was accorded to that letter. The word applause does not describe the expression which followed its reading. It was something much more profound and significant than that. It was applause indeed, but it had an undertone full of the deepest melody and the most touching pathos. It was plainly distinguishable. It was the spontaneous, hearty expression of the love of the bar of Cincinnati for Rufus King. I do not doubt but in that moment there came to the mind of each one present that which came to my own mind—the painful thought that this gifted, useful, honorable life was drawing to a close. His loss is irreparable in a large and true sense. Let us cherish his memory. Let us emulate, so far as we can, his virtues. Let us serve our fellow-men according to the utmost of our ability, for the love of God.

Ex-Governor Cox's Tribute.

Ex-Governor Cox then spoke. During much of the time since the war, ex-Governor Cox has been closely associated with Mr. King in the Law School. His tribute was to Mr. King's peculiar fitness as an instructor, his keen analytical power, his solid and robust treatment of such subjects as constitutional law, the lucid way in which he brought his reasoning home to his pupils. He was a man who never exhibited despondency, but was always bouyant in spirit, gracious in demeanor, unselfish—one who recognized his duties toward the community and was laborious in their performance when it could be done without reward. Modest in all things concerning his own work, yet fully aware that he possessed a faculty for doing it, he was possessed of all the elements which go to make a noble character.

Ex-Judge Avery on his Public Work.

Ex-Judge Avery confined himself largely to Mr. King's unostentatious but most fruitful work in behalf of the public—his long connection with the public schools, and the large part he had in the founding of the Law Library, the Public Library, the Art Museum, the building of Music Hall, the important work of the tax commission, the deliberations of the constitutional convention, and the management of the University of Cincinnati. While president of the school board, to which he was elected for many years from a ward of opposite politics from his own, his work was not only that of a presiding officer, for which he had rare fitness, but also included a large amount of labor which now devolves upon the superintendent. Mr. King's reports while president of the school board were quoted from freely in proof that he was the directing head and hand and heart which brought the Cincinnati public schools up to the high standard of efficiency which in later years has been accorded to them. Mr. King had no children of his own living, but the children of the public schools were his by adoption, and profited from his anxious care extended over a long period. In speaking of Mr. King's work in connection with the collection of the Law and Public Libraries, ex-Judge Avery laid special stress on his penchant for the collection of old pamphlets relating to early times and local history. The stores of these pamphlets which are now in the libraries through Mr. King's efforts are of the greatest value, and so rare that of many of them it would now be impossible to supply duplicates.

Judge Hunt's Tribute.

The Hon. Samuel F. Hunt was then introduced by Aaron F. Perry, President of the meeting. He said that Judge Hunt had been an attached friend of Rufus King, and as presiding judge of the Superior Court, he had been selected as one who should say a word on this occasion.

Judge Hunt said no member of the bar had passed the gates of death crowned with so many honorable years as Rufus King. There was something in his face not unlike the received image of those who lingered about the Academy—of the friend of whom Xenophon spoke in his affectionate language as "the one who handled all with whom he conversed just as he pleased."

He spake as a thoughtful and conscientious man, from the conviction of his own judgment. His opinions commanded respect and deference and carried with them a corresponding weight and influence. His whole life, private, professional, and public, was devoted to the public good. No man ever left a more honorable record. His intellectual endowments were happily blended with the kindliest affections of heart, and above all these could be recognized the sublime graces of a consistent

Christian character. He had withal the spirit of humanity of which only Christianity can furnish a parallel. He felt like Newton that he had gathered only a few shells on the great sea-shore. He recognized that the egotism of man must give way to the presence of the Adorable. Like Moses, he would have put off his shoes as he approached holy ground. His spirit never stooped to littleness nor meanness of action. He spent many years among the monarchs of thought. He rejoiced in the sparkling crests and mists of the ocean, but he saw the immense sublimity of the infinity of waters beneath.

Judge Hunt said that those who planted the foundations of human learning should have great honor and be the world's high priests, going into the most holy places. Rufus King emphasized the idea that the public schools should be the schools for the people, and he gave them that high character which is still a cherished tradition. Rufus King prepared the McMicken University bill with Dr. Comegys on which the present Cincinnati University is founded. He realized that Cincinnati should give a splendid patronage to learning. He believed in affording privileges to the youth of the city in the direction of a culture which would not only enrich the city of their birth, but which would bestow upon the country an act in harmony with its advanced civilization.

The Art Museum, which crowns our hills like the majestic Parthenon on the Acropolis, is largely the result of the patient thought and attentive industry of Rufus King in the original school of art and design in Cincinnati.

Judge Hunt then referred to the abiding attachment which had been awakened by their association in the university board and as members of the third constitutional convention of Ohio. His home life was delightful. He worshiped his household gods. The sweetest incense daily arose from his domestic altars. In the social gatherings of his home during the sitting of the convention in Cincinnati,

Dean Swift would have been a welcome guest, who could have appreciated the wit and repartee of his genial host. Judge Hunt referred to the words of Lord Mansfield, in which he said that there was nothing more desirable in life than the consciousness of an honest endeavor for the acquisition of honorable fame. The ancestry of Rufus King entitled him to insignia and coronets, but he preferred the title which comes not of lineage and insignia and coronets, but which comes from the consciousness of duty well done. He was the crowned citizen, because he filled the whole measure of citizenship. It was that conviction which makes the whole city to-day regard and regret the loss of this man. Judge Hunt then closed with the hope that the name of Rufus King would stand as the gentleman, as the kindly, dignified man, as the self-sacrificing citizen, as the one of absolute integrity, as one who could not be turned from the path of honor. He bore that name which is better than great riches, and held it stainless to the last.

Mr. Groesbeck's Tribute.

Hon. Wm. S. Groesbeck said, on being called to his feet by the chairman, that he felt no inclination to speak. He was there to pay his profound respect to the memory of Rufus King. What he would say of him would not be of his career as a lawyer, but as a citizen and as a man—an excellent, honorable, exemplary man, who did not live in vain. He was the most valuable citizen, said Mr. Groesbeck, that Cincinnati ever had. There is no need for exaggeration. His life can be contemplated just as it was. It is astonishing that amid the duties of his profession he could find time to do so much that was for the public good. He gave years and years and years to the service of the people, but the doors of the public treasury never opened to him.

A Letter from Ex-Governor Hoadly.

A letter expressive of the general loss in the death of Mr. King, written by ex-Governor Hoadly upon receipt of news of his death, was read by Mr. Brannan. He became acquainted, he said, with Mr. King forty-five years ago, in the office of Salmon P. Chase, once a partner of Mr. King's father. No one knows better than I, said the ex-governor, how great the loss which the bar of Cincinnati and the cause of sound legal principles for which it stands have met in the decease of our lamented friend. Continuing, the distinguished writer spoke of Mr. King as the only true Federalist he had ever known—the best representative of that ambition for highly developed but honest government for which the Federal party stood. Speaking of the high places in political life Mr. King might have attained and filled with credit had his views been more attached to either of the great parties, the ex-governor closed with the significant remark, "that it would have been unimportant, however, in comparison with the great example of public spirit, legal learning, and domestic virtue which he has set before our eyes for half a century."

CINCINNATI LAW LIBRARY.

Memorial adopted by the Board, March 26, 1891.

RUFUS KING.

We mourn because we have lost Rufus King, whose many years were all rich with usefulness and bright with honors which came unsought. Although he preferred the regard of those around him to the cold glitter of wider fame, he kept the promise of a distinguished lineage and met the obligations of a great name. He was one of those men who enrich any community where they live, because they belong to it every way and always. He shirked no duty. He neglected no trust. He never wearied in fidelity to truth and right. The law was to him a learned, humane and honorable profession, in which gain never supplanted justice. Life was to him only a succession of opportunities to do good. We can ill spare any good man, worst of all the few, among whom he was pre-eminent, who have the inclination and the ability and can find the time throughout busy lives to do those duties which make no appeal to selfishness or vanity, but whose doing keeps alive intelligence and morality in public and private life.

Mr. King's long connection with the Cincinnati Law Library Association makes it fitting for us, as its board of trustees, to express the esteem and gratitude of the association. He was one of its founders, its president for nearly forty years, its constant friend and benefactor. By his aid and efforts more than by those of any other member, the library rose from its ashes. Under his wise management, it has been through all these years a pride, a help, and an inspiration to the lawyers of Cincinnati.

Rufus King could have no better monument to his memory, if monument were needed, than the thousands of volumes whose silent array holds and perpetuates the noble science he loved so well.

MEMORIAL OF MR. KING.

Prepared by Ex-Governor Cox.

ADOPTED BY THE TRUSTEES OF THE CINCINNATI COLLEGE AT THEIR MEETING ON THE 2D OF APRIL, 1891.

HON. RUFUS KING,
LATE PROFESSOR IN THE CINCINNATI LAW SCHOOL.

In the death of Rufus King, of Cincinnati, the bar throughout the country will be sensible of a serious loss. Although nearly seventy-four years of age when he died on the 25th of March, he had continued his active work with uncommon vigor of body and mind down to November last. He had begun his usual course of lectures on the principles of constitutional law at the opening of the term of the Cincinnati Law School, with which he had been connected for many years, but what seemed a temporary illness interrupted his teaching. He and his colleagues hoped still he would soon return to his favorite work, and it was not until within a few days of his death that it became evident his life's work was done.

Mr. King was an admirable example of the thoroughly equipped lawyer, devoted to his profession, and steadily giving himself up to its private practice despite many and frequent temptations to enter public life. Of this class in the profession, very few in any part of the country are known better than he—west of the Alleghany mountains, none, it is safe to say, who have declined political and judicial honors, have had a more solid professional career, or can more truly be regarded as the type of the highly intellectual, refined, and able lawyer, scrupulously consecrating his hours and his strength to strictly professional work, except as he, with equal scrupulousness, performed the quiet duties of a private citizen in the various walks of local charities, educational advancement, and diocesan church work. Mr. King was grandson of Rufus King, the distinguished Federalist statesman of New York in the revolutionary and constitution-forming period of the national history, and inherited some of the most marked mental and moral characteristics of that great man. He had the same broad grasp of fundamental principles in law and in politics; the same devotion to true republicanism in government, tempered by the same conservatism. He believed with all his heart in the nationality of the federal union, and desired to preserve it by interpreting its constitutional powers so as to give it true national strength and vigor. He had the high sense of honor which lifted him above even the temptation to self-seeking and gave him a standard of public and private honesty which made him an acknowledged model for all about him. Without the slightest assumption or artificiality of conduct, he had a natural and simple dignity of the truest polish and most excellent taste, because it was the outward exhibition of a modest, a refined, and an earnestly benevolent nature. With all this, he had the courage of his convictions, and whether as advocate or as citizen, he knew how to meet with vigor and to combat unflinchingly every aggression against the right. In every duty and in every place he carried with him the manifest evidence of transparent purity of purpose and chivalrous devotion, and when the charm of his personal manners was added, he appeared to be what he was, the thorough Christian gentleman, as felicitous in the form of action as in the action itself.

On both sides of the house Mr. King came of excellent American stock. His mother was the daughter of Governor Worthington, who was of the Virginia colony in Ohio, settling at Chillicothe, the first capital of the state, in the midst of the Scioto lands allotted by Virginia before the cession to her revolutionary soldiers. The Kings were of the New England colony before they became New Yorkers, and so the best northern blood and southern blood mingled in his veins. His father, Edward King, had left New York a young man to see what opening fortune might offer him as a lawyer in the new State of Ohio. Visiting Governor Worthington's family, he found attractions in Chillicothe which fastened him, for there he wooed and wedded Sarah Worthington, and won also an early success at the bar as an eloquent and accomplished lawyer.

When the capital of the state was removed from Ross county to Columbus, the Kings changed their home to Cincinnati, where the largest field offered itself to a lawyer of recognized power.

Mr. Edward King, Judge John C. Wright, and Mr. Timothy Walker established the Cincinnati Law School in 1833—the first attempt at systematic legal education in the Mississippi valley. Mr. Rufus King's great interest in the Law School was therefore hereditary, like his virtues. After preparing for and beginning his collegiate education at Kenyon College, Bishop Chase's new foundation, he completed his undergraduate course at Harvard University, taking his degree of B. A. there in 1839. Mr. King remained at Cambridge in the Dane Law School, under Story and Greenleaf, through a two years' course, graduating in 1840, and returned home to Cincinnati to practice his profession. His junior partners in practice constitute a long line of men in the first rank of political, judicial, and professional eminence. He himself, however, adhered to his purpose to remain a private citizen except when, in 1874, he became a member of the convention to revise the constitution of the state. This was so eminently a call to the highest work of the lawyer, that he yielded to it; and after Morrison R. Waite was transferred from its chair to the chief-justiceship of the Supreme Court of the United States, Mr. King was his successor in the presidency of the convention. He did not shrink from the labor of administering local interests, especially educational. He was long active in the board of directors of the public schools; he was the chief actor in creating the Cincinnati Public Library; he was one of the first trustees of the McMicken bequest and for many years nursed it into the foundation of the University of Cincinnati. In 1875, the trustees of the old corporation of the Cincinnati College, incorporated in 1819, determined to enlarge the course of study in the Law School, and Mr. King became the dean of the faculty, with the arrangement that he should retire from active practice in court and devote most of his time to the school. He took upon himself the burden of instructing the junior class daily in the elements and institutes, besides lecturing to the senior class in one department of the law. In connection with this, he continued his consultation and chamber practice, but after five years asked to be relieved from the deanship, resuming full practice and continuing his lectures on constitutional law and the law of real property. In these professional relations his last years were spent, and though he was relieved from the more severe labors of the court-room and of the office, he kept the harness on till his last sickness overtook him. In 1888, he wrote for the American Commonwealth Series his historical volume on "Ohio, the First Fruits of the Ordinance of 1787." This is chiefly devoted to the analysis of the events which led to and accompanied the organization of Ohio as a state and gave character to the new community. The picture of western civilization and of the elements and forces co-operating to make the new state what it was, is ably and attractively drawn. The bent of the mind of the constitutional lawyer is seen in each step of the historian's work, and gives broader scope and value to a narrative that is singularly lucid and often even picturesque.

Mr. King was always an active member of the Bar Association of the state, and for many years a prominent figure, also, in the meetings of the National Bar Association. In the meeting of the bar which crowded the United States court-room in Cincinnati to express sorrow at his death, the key-note was well struck by the Hon. William S. Groesbeck, who said, that with all his professional activities and valuable labors as a professor of law, Mr. King would best be remembered by his friends and neighbors as the model citizen, using his legal knowledge and business acumen to aid every good cause, to foster every local improvement, to advance education in all departments, and to befriend every man and woman needing the counsel and assistance of a large-hearted and able friend.

STUDENTS OF THE LAW SCHOOL.

Whereas, The Supreme Judge of the Universe has in His wisdom summoned our exemplar and instructor, Rufus King, to a higher court.

Resolved, That in the death of Professor King the Law School of the Cincinnati College loses an able, efficient, and enthusiastic officer, and the students an earnest and sympathizing friend. As dean, and later as professor of real property and constitutional law, he gave the college the benefit of his rare executive ability, valuable experience, and ripened scholarship. The long line of students who came under his instruction found his true culture, vigorous personality, and sterling manhood a perpetual aid and encouragement in their professional aspirations.

Resolved, That we, the class of '91 of the

Cincinnati Law School, express to the family of Mr. King our heartfelt sympathy in this great bereavement, and the hope that his influence may long be continued in the lives of the young men who will strive to follow his example.

G. GLENN ATKINS,
ELLIS GUY KINCAID,
THOMAS MORAN,
Committee.

March 26, 1891.

TRUSTEES OF THE DIOCESE OF SOUTHERN OHIO.

The trustees of the Protestant Episcopal Church in the diocese of Southern Ohio desire to record their sense of the great loss which they and the diocese they represent have sustained in the death of Rufus King, who for many years has been the honored president of the board. Always prompt and faithful in the discharge of every duty, Mr. King gave to the interests of the diocese the advantage of his great learning and assiduous care, while his kindness and courtesy endeared him to his associates and to all with whom his official duties brought him into contact. His loss will long be mourned. His place can not be filled.

LARZ ANDERSON,
Secretary.

CINCINNATI, *March* 28, 1891.

ST. PAUL'S CHURCH.

At a meeting of the rector, wardens, and vestry of St. Paul's Church, duly convened, the following minutes were unanimously adopted and ordered to be spread upon the records upon a page especially devoted to the purpose:

IN MEMORIAM.

We, the rector, wardens, and vestry of the church, desire to place in permanent form the expression of our affectionate memory of our late associate, the Hon. Rufus King, and our deep grief at the great loss which, in his recent death on the 25th ult., we, our church and congregation, as well as the whole community, have sustained.

Mr. King had been for fifty years identified with this parish, and was at his death the oldest member of the congregation. He was elected vestryman in 1847, and served as a faithful and efficient member of the vestry for thirty-six consecutive years. His sound sense, clear judgment, wise counsels, were to us of eminent value, and his gentle manners, firm principles, and uniform courtesy greatly endeared him to us, as to all with whom he was associated. We feel his loss deeply, remembering his fidelity, his sagacity, his ready and efficient personal services at all periods in our history, especially at the time of our late removal, and his zeal and liberality since in extinguishing the last indebtedness of the parish, placing our endowment on a firm basis.

In honor of his person and character, in gratitude for his services, in loving memory of his virtues, we, his associates and successors in the vestry of St. Paul's Church, while deploring the loss which the parish and the whole diocese have sustained, desire to give expression to our profound and affectionate appreciation of his long and devout attend ance on the services of the church and unfailing and large-hearted Christian liberality. The influence of such an example is invaluable and will long endure.

Easter Monday, 1891.

KENYON COLLEGE.

At a meeting of the board of trustees of Kenyon College, held in Gambier, June 26, 1891, a committee, consisting of Bishop Vincent, the Rev. Mr. Rhodes, and the Hon. Channing Richards, was appointed to draw up and present a suitable minute concerning the Hon. Rufus King, a late member of this board, of which minute the following is a copy :

"In view of the long and faithful services of the Hon. Rufus King as a member of the board, and his deep interest in the institutions at Gambier, this board has received with deep sorrow the announcement of his death, and now records its appreciation of his high character and distinguished services in the cause of liberal education, both here and elsewhere.

TRUSTEES OF THOMAS HUGHES'S WILL.

Since our last meeting, death has taken from us our dear friend and president of the trust,

RUFUS KING.

The eulogies which have been pronounced elsewhere, graceful tributes as they have been, did not exaggerate his character—true man and Christian gentleman, faithful to all trusts, earnest for the public good.

Whatever rewards are reserved for duty performed and a life well spent, he will have entered into their full fruition. We mourn the loss of our friend and colleague, and shall ever cherish his memory.

The above was unanimously adopted at a special meeting of the trustees of the Thomas

Hughes will, held April 15, 1891. Ordered to be spread upon the minutes.

B. O. M. DeBECK,
Secretary.

SOCIAL SCIENCE.

"At the session of the Department of Jurisprudence of this association at the annual meeting at Saratoga, September 3, 1891, the chairman of the department, Professor Wayland, presiding, it was voted, upon the announcement of Mr. King's death, that a brief memoir of him be prepared by the secretary for the journal of Social Science." In accordance with that vote, a memoir was written, giving a sketch of Mr. King's life and work, closing with the following tribute:

"Such, in his relation to the city of his abode, was the member of our association whose loss we deplore; and to such men, of public service and of private virtues, the work of social science most naturally falls in our country. Had he been ambitious of political honors, he would not, for so many years, have cast in his lot with those who aspire to no political office, though ready to perform the duties of any station to which they may be called. His was the distinction, among a people who seek the emoluments as well as the honors of office, steadfastly to decline salaried positions, and to render that unpaid service to his fellow-citizens which our system in its perfection requires. He took part in our meetings at Cincinnati in 1878, and for many years in Saratoga, because he liked to hear what earnest thinkers had to say, and was ready to add his judicious and well-considered word. The ornament of the bar, he was no less the ornament of any assembly in which he took part— a clear reasoner, a modest proposer of useful truth, and a seconder of whatever was beneficial to the country and the world. He might have filled the stations to which his ancestors were called; for he was a senatorial person, and, as Horace said of his friend, and Milton of John Bradshaw, *consul non unius anni*. But he chose the more quiet path of liberal studies and professional eminence; and it was his delight to give the hospitality of his house and of his mind to those who had the pleasure of his acquaintance, with Horatian ease and with Christian generosity. In all this he was happily seconded by the wife of his youth, who survives him, and to whom all who knew Mr. King accord that sympathy which is the best offering of human nature in such a bereavement.

F. B. S.

CONCORD, *November* 4, 1891.

COLLEGE OF MUSIC.

IN MEMORIAM.

RUFUS KING.

To the community which for half a century has regarded Rufus King as one of its foremost citizens, the announcement of his death brought peculiar and poignant sorrow. Words are inadequate to express the emotion with which all that is mortal of so good and great a man is laid away to rest until the great awakening.

What he was in his public life, the annals of his native state attest; what he was in his chosen profession of the law, the bench and bar of Ohio know full well; what he was as a private citizen, the thousands who in his adopted city have enjoyed the fruits of his judicious counsel and untiring labor clearly understand; what he was as a friend, those who have known him intimately now realize with the keenness born of loss.

What he was as a son and husband, will never be fully known on earth. In all the positions that he occupied during an eventful life, he was an unostentatious, honorable Christian gentlemen, eminently fitted by his birth, his education, and his abilities for the exalted station in society to which he so naturally attained. In the providence of God, his virtues are not transmitted to any immediate descendants. He honorably maintained a name which has for generations been a synonym for patriotism, noble ambition, and eminent success.

The trustees of the College of Music of Cincinnati pay this tribute to the memory of a man who was one of its founders and most devoted friends. They hope that the memory of his manly virtues will incite many of his fellow-citizens to emulate his noble life; and they cherish the assurance that

"The memory of the just is blessed."

IN MEMORY OF
THE HON. RUFUS KING.

Office of Spring Grove Cemetery,
March 26, 1891.

At the special meeting of the directors, called this morning to express their sense of the great loss they have suffered, in common with the lot-owners, in the death of the late Hon. Rufus King, they have directed the following minute to be placed on the records of the association :

As fellow-trustees with Mr. King for many years, it is proper we should express our sorrow that these official relations which had ripened into tender personal friendships have been severed. In 1878, in consequence of the death of his intimate friend, Mr. Larz Anderson, whom he succeeded in the board, he entered upon his duties here—congenial duties, not to be relinquished till his life's end. He regarded it as a trust requiring his consideration, being present at every meeting as his rule. To this service he gave much time and thought taken from the cares of an exacting profession. Can too much be said of the value of the service given by him in his later years, so full of knowledge in its wider range, the habit of legal examination, accurate reasoning, a broad, generous spirit in discussion, ever courteous and gentlemanly in manner? Mr. King possessed one of those exalted natures in which lives a noble, liberal soul that influences the conduct of his fellow-men and diffuses sweet influences every-where. His kindly voice and genial manner will live, and one might say "that to serve God and be cheerful" was his motto. No insincerity nor meanness, no jealousy or selfishness, found place in his heart. He came forth every morning fresh to duty year by year, unharmed by anxious care, unsoiled by the ceaseless greed for gain that tempts so many to forfeit honor and virtue.

With such qualities, governed by principle that would scorn a doubtful action, he yet rejoiced in such universal friendship that he may be said to have left no enemies. Our honored and beloved friend was privileged to attain the fullness of years, but now this almost perfect life, so rich, so complete, so full of priceless example, is ended on earth, for as yesterday's early dawn awoke nature to a new day, God's finger touched him, the angel turned the gates aside, and his spirit entered the portals of Paradise in his sleep.

By order of the board of directors.

HENRY PROBASCO,
President.

JOE C. SPEAR.
Secretary.

www.ingramcontent.com/pod-product-compliance
Lightning Source LLC
Chambersburg PA
CBHW020134170426
43199CB00010B/742